*THIS BOOK HAS BEEN DISCARDED
BY SKULL ISLAND PUBLIC LIBRARY*

GIANT APES
OF THE MOVIES
By John LeMay

Copyright © 2020 by Bicep Books.

All images reproduced within this book derive from memorabilia, publicity photos, and other publicity materials. This material appears here for the sole purpose of publicity and education. The publisher also wishes to acknowledge that they claim no rights to the underlying artistic works, photos, or images embodied in this book.

GIANT APES
OF THE MOVIES

GUYS IN APE SUITS

It was the great filmmaker John Landis who once said that he "loved any movie with a guy in an ape suit." In fact, he loved them so much he climbed into an ape suit himself and made the movie *SCHLOCK!* in 1973. The film was part of a long line of camp classics about gorillas loose in civilization, wreaking havoc, and abducting beautiful women.

Of course, we all know where that came from. Does the image of a huge gorilla scaling a building with a pretty girl in his grasp come to mind? It should. But no, it's not King Kong! This concept actually originated in the 1932 adaptation of *Murders in the Rue Morgue*.

Bela Lugosi in Murders in the Rue Morgue *(1932).*

Still from the climax of Murders in the Rue Morgue *(see the ape on the right).*

In the story, originally written by Edgar Allen Poe in 1841, a mad scientist named Dr. Mirakle injects kidnapped women with the blood of his caged ape! Dr. Mirakle was portrayed by none other than Bela Lugosi, who had played Dracula only the year before. At the picture's climax, the caged ape escapes and climbs to the roof of the house with a beautiful woman in his grasp. *King Kong* would come out the very next year, in 1933.

Even before that, damsels being carried off by apes turned up in artwork from the Victorian Era and the Great War periods. To go back even further in history, western civilization wasn't introduced to the concept of the ape until the 1860s. They were first discovered by the American physician and missionary Thomas Staughton Savage. Actually, all he found at the time were their bones in Liberia, Africa. The first explorer to actually see a live gorilla was Paul Du Chaillu in western equatorial Africa, which he explored from 1856 to 1859. In 1861, he shocked western civilization by bringing to London the dead body of a great ape. Even in the very early 1900s, apes were still a mysterious animal for most people, and they weren't studied in depth until the 1920s. Carl Akeley, of the American Museum of Natural History, went to Africa in the hopes of capturing a specimen. It seems that apes and adventure stories have always been tied together; with Akeley on the trip was Mary Bradley, a mystery writer. After the trip was over, she would even write a book about it called *On the Gorilla Trail*. With her was her husband, and also their daughter Alice. As it turned out, Alice would grow up to be a science fiction writer. But, since publishers were afraid that stories written by a woman wouldn't sell well, her stories were published under the pen name of "James Tiptree Jr."!

So perhaps we should not be surprised by the close connection between beauties, beasts, and adventure stories.

Drawing of French explorer Paul Du Chaillu at close quarters with a gorilla.

Rare still from The Perils of Pauline *(left), and the 1927 version of* The Gorilla *(right).*

THE FIRST APE SUIT MOVIES

Before King Kong, brought to life via a stop-motion model, the very first ape movies used men in suits. The first ape suit on film is believed to have debuted in an episode of *The Perils of Pauline* serial from 1914. Specifically, it showed up in Chapter 20, though we don't know what actually happened in the story, as that particular episode was lost. But, thanks to a researcher named Craig Scott Lamb, a few stills were at least uncovered from the project.

The next ape suit movie that we can find comes 13 years later: 1927's *The Gorilla*. The film is literally about a man in an ape suit committing murders. It was likely inspired in part by Edgar Allen Poe's *Murders in the Rue Morgue*, but the film was for certain based upon a play by Ralph Spence.

The movie was shot silent, as talking pictures were still uncommon (actually, the first, called *The Jazz Singer*, was released that same year!). The movie starred Charles Murray, Fred Kelsey, and Walter Pidgeon. *The Gorilla* would be remade not once, but twice. The first remake, from 1930 (and with sound this time), was again titled *The Gorilla*. The movie starts out with a giant ape lumbering through a city. But don't get too excited. That's not what the movie is actually about. Once again, it's about a criminal nicknamed the gorilla, the credits were just done for dramatic effect. Still, thanks to the credit scene, *The Gorilla* beat *King Kong* by three years as the first movie to have a giant ape walk through a city. The next remake, from 1939, was this time a comedy starring the Ritz brothers and also featured Bela Lugosi.

In the film's story, a killer targets a rich mansion owner, who calls in three private eyes (the Ritz brothers) to protect him. At the same time, the killer has hired a trainer and his pet gorilla to go to the mansion to "put on a show for a party." The gorilla is then loosed upon the mansion about halfway through the film and hilarity ensues.

The man inhabiting the ape suit in many of these old movies was Carlos "Charles" Gemora, born on June 15, 1903. Gemora was a Hollywood make-up artist who created gorilla suits and also wore them on film. In fact, as the years went on, Gemora would eventually be nicknamed "the King of the Gorilla Men" due to his many appearances in Hollywood movies wearing ape suits.

Charles Gemora, the famous ape suit performer.

King Kong Made in Japan *(1933)*.

KING KONG IN JAPAN

Long before Godzilla ever terrorized the silver screen, Japanese special effects technicians first created their own version of *King Kong*. However, this was no "rip-off," but a tie-in comical short set to accompany the Japanese dubbed release of *King Kong* in Japan. The short film, *King Kong Made in Japan*, was made by Shochiku.

The story concerned two unemployed, homeless men, Santa and Koichi. Santa has a girlfriend, Omitsu, whom he wants to marry, but Omitsu's father wants to marry her off to a rich man. Noticing the successful release of *King Kong* in Japan, Santa gets the crazy idea to portray Kong in an ape suit in his own vaudeville production. The show, wherein Santa trashes various miniatures in his Kong suit, is a runaway hit. One night, Omitsu attends with her new boyfriend, whom Santa attacks in his Kong suit. Santa chases the man outside the theater creating a furor in the streets resulting in the fire department and police called out. Santa knocks out the boyfriend and then places him in the ape suit. However, all ends well as the theater owner tells Santa he will pay him lots of money to keep reprising his role as King Kong. Santa, now rich, marries Omitsu.

In 1938 came another "King Kong" movie called *King Kong Appears in Edo*. It wasn't really about King Kong though, but a normal-sized ape named King Kong. The story was set in Feudal Japan and concerned the daughter of a wealthy landowner getting kidnapped by the villain's pet ape, King Kong. In the end, the girl is rescued, and King Kong kills his villainous owner.

Sadly, this film and *King Kong Made in Japan* were destroyed in the bombing of Hiroshima in World War II.

Despite his giant stature on the poster, "King Kong" remains normal-sized throughout King Kong Appears in Edo *(1938).*

John Carradine in Captive Wild Woman (1943)

GORILLAS ON THE LOOSE

After the huge success of *King Kong* in 1933, the public continued to be fascinated by ape movies. But there was one problem. The animation method used to bring Kong to life was both costly and took a long time. Movie producers wanted their movies out fast and cheap, so to create their gorillas they turned to, what else, men in suits.

Universal, the studio famous for Classic Monsters like Frankenstein, Dracula, the Mummy, and the Wolf Man, shot a movie in 1943 called *Captive Wild Woman*. You could say the movie was similar to *The Wolf Man*, only, in this case, a beautiful girl turns into a gorilla!

This transformation isn't due to a curse, but the experiments of a mad scientist, Dr. Walters (John Carradine). Walters steals a female gorilla, named Cheela, from a circus. Dr. Walters then combines the DNA of a woman with Cheela, who transforms into a beautiful girl! But the woman still behaves like an animal, so Walters transplants the brain of his female assistant into the new body, which he names Paula. This new woman appears to be normal, but one day an accident occurs at the circus. An animal trainer is attacked by lions. Paula runs into the cage and frightens the animals away to everyone's shock. As the story progresses, Paula reverts back to the animal form of Cheela, necessitating more experiments on the part of Dr. Walters.

In the end, the experiments are unsuccessful, and Cheela is killed by the police. But, Cheela didn't stay dead for long. Cheela/Paula returned for two sequels: *Jungle Woman* (1944) *and Jungle Captive* (1945).

Lobby card for Nabonga *(1944).*

The year 1944 brought with it the movie *Nabonga*, another 'beauty and the beast' tale, this one focusing on a pretty girl named Doreen protected by a large gorilla. The male lead is played by actor Buster Crabbe. His character, Ray Gorman, travels to Africa to clear his deceased father's name of embezzlement. In the jungle he finds the daughter of the real embezzler: Doreen (Julie London in her first film) also called the 'White Witch'. To make things complicated, Doreen, who doesn't want to give up the money, is guarded by a large gorilla,

Samson. However, in the end, Samson turns into a hero when he defends Ray and Doreen from a villain on their trail and Doreen decides to give the money back.

The movie is padded with the usual jungle stock footage featuring people getting chased by crocodiles while swimming across rivers, gorillas fighting to the death, and so on. The film was shot in 1943 but wasn't released until the following year. Perhaps wanting to get some more mileage out of the gorilla suit, the producers would follow

Scene from **White Pongo** *(1945).*

this film with *White Pongo* the very next year.

The story focused on an expedition searching for a white gorilla that is somehow "the missing link." The film is padded out with stock shots of jungle wildlife, including Komodo Dragons, which most certainly do not hail from Africa. In fact, most of the film is comprised of lengthy shots of the characters paddling upriver. The ape does the usual King Kong impression and abducts the female starlet and at one point plucks off her necklace. For that matter, the White Pongo suit and the supporting gorilla suits aren't bad at all for 1945, they just needed a more exciting script to perform for. The only excitement in the whole film occurs when White Pongo battles another gorilla over the female lead. The film ends with the White Pongo captured and ready to be taken to civilization. Perhaps the producers were hoping for a sequel?

After *White Pongo* came *The White Gorilla*. This might be one of the earliest examples of a 'Frankenmovie.' What's that you ask? A Franken-movie, which alludes to Frankenstein, refers to the case of footage from an old movie being used as the basis for a new one. In this case, most of the footage came from the 1927 silent film *Perils of the Jungle*. The new footage, shot over the course of only three days and one night in 1945, existed solely to prop up the more exciting, and noticeably different, footage from 1927.

The story is told via a narrator, who walks into a trading post beaten and disheveled by a legendary white ape and the man explains his various adventures in the jungle. This narrator relates his flashbacks with total seriousness, which is unintentionally funny considering he never interacts with the noticeably older footage.

Of the title character, the white gorilla has been ostracized by all the black gorillas. Angry due to being shunned, he terrorizes various hunters. In the end, he faces off against the king of the gorillas as "the fate of Africa hangs in the balance."

One of the most fun "giant ape" movies of all time doesn't technically even contain a giant ape. The film is called *Unknown Island* and was shot in vibrant Cinecolor in 1948. It tells the familiar story of explorers looking for an island of dinosaurs. They find the island, the dinosaurs, and a giant sloth—which easily looks more like a giant ape than a sloth. The climax of the film has the hairy animal battle a T-Rex in something of a precursor/poor man's version of *King Kong vs. Godzilla* (1962). The duel to the death is surprisingly violent for 1948 standards, and each monster bites out a chunk of the other. In the end, the "giant sloth" emerges as the victor.

Due to the film having no copyright, footage from it showed up in other movies down the road, notably *Gigantis, the Fire Monster* (1959).

Before Kong fought Godzilla, this T-Rex and this giant sloth fought to the death in Unknown Island *(1948).*

Lou Costello and friend in **Africa Screams** *(1949).*

In 1949, after having "met" Frankenstein, Abbott and Costello met a giant ape in *Africa Screams*. Not surprisingly, it's rumored that this movie started out as "Abbott and Costello Meet King Kong"!

Africa Screams is one of the better Abbott and Costello films. In it, the duo poses as big game hunters when, in fact, they are just book store clerks who have read about big game hunters. The two join an expedition looking for a giant ape, the Orangutan Gargantuan, to Africa (which is just a ruse for the villains looking for lost diamonds). As it turns out the diamonds and the ape both exist!

Over the course of the film, Costello's character accidentally saves a juvenile Orangutan Gargantuan putting him forever in the ape's debt. At the picture's end, just as the bad guys have Costello cornered, the giant ape steps behind Costello and frightens the men off (though Costello thinks that he himself has frightened them off!). Once again, the giant ape was played by none other than Charles Gemora.

The year 1951 brought *Bride of the Gorilla*, which was somewhat similar to *Captive Wild Woman*. In this case, a plantation worker in the jungle named Chavez (played by Raymond Burr) has a curse placed on him by a native woman. Chavez then becomes a were-gorilla! If this sounds familiar to *The Wolf Man* (1941), that's because this movie was made by *Wolf Man* writer Curt Siodmak.

Barbara Payton in the grasp of the gorilla in **The Bride of the Gorilla** *(1945).*

Still from Bela Lugosi Meets a Brooklyn Gorilla *(1952)*.

The next year came another comedy in the form of *Bela Lugosi Meets a Brooklyn Gorilla* (1952). The movie's original title was to be "White Woman of the Lost Jungle" until the producer changed it to exploit Lugosi's name. Other than Lugosi, the movie starred a comedy duo named Duke Mitchell and Sammy Petrillo, who imitated the better-known duo of Dean Martin and Jerry Lewis. Lugosi plays a mad scientist, Dr. Zabor, while Mitchell and Petrillo play a couple of entertainers that fall out of their airplane and become stranded on Zabor's island. Dr. Zabor is conducting 'evolutionary' experiments on gorillas and chimpanzees via growth serum. The serum ends up turning Mitchell's character into the titular Brooklyn Gorilla. This is where most of the film's humor is generated, particularly when a real gorilla is mistaken for the intelligent Mitchell's gorilla by Petrillo. In the end, the whole story turns out to be Petrillo's backstage dream.

KONGA

Of all the giant apes other than King Kong, Konga, star of the 1961 film of the same name, is probably the best known. Unlike many gorilla movies of the past few years that featured normal-sized apes, *Konga* featured a giant chimpanzee (even though it looks just like a gorilla)! The movie was produced by Herman Cohen, and started out with the crazy title of "I Was a Teenaged Gorilla"! But, Cohen wanted to reference King Kong in the title and came up with the name "Konga." To do so, he paid Kong's owners, RKO, a fee of $25,000.

The story of *Konga* revolves around Dr. Charles Decker (Michael Gough), who returns to civilization after a year long research trip to Africa. With him are his precious pet chimp, Konga, and a bunch of carnivorous plants. Decker makes a secret growth formula out of the plants which he injects into baby Konga. The ape soon grows larger with each injection, and Decker uses the giant chimp to murder his enemies and colleagues. But, eventually, Konga grabs Decker and walks through downtown London causing people to panic where he is shot and killed by the military. Decker is killed when the ape throws him to the ground.

Otango, the giant ape in Shikari *(1963) terrorizes a village.*

KING KONG GOES TO INDIA

Over in India, in what many jokingly refer to Bollywood, or India's version of Hollywood, a quasi-remake of *King Kong* crossed with *Dr. Cyclops* (1940) was made called *Shikari* in 1963. The plot is said to revolve around a circus company travelling into the jungle to capture a giant ape called Otango. On their journey, they run into the evil Dr. Cyclops, who it turns out, created the giant ape.

Scenes of Otango wrecking the native village are quite fun, though it should be noted that the giant ape isn't in the film for long. In fact, after he wrecks the village, he falls into a river of lava! Despite its low budget, the film was a big hit at the box office, and songs for the film likewise became big hits in India.

Scene from the climax of Tarzan and King Kong *(1965).*

Two years later, Bollywood produced *Tarzan and King Kong*. The idea of pitting King Kong against Tarzan was actually pitched back in 1934 for a movie that ended up not getting made. Unfortunately, this Bollywood version isn't that exciting. Furthermore, the "King Kong" referred to in the title is actually just a human wrestler that Tarzan must defeat!

Further confusing the matter is that a villainous gorilla also appears—not named King Kong. When the gorilla kidnaps Tarzan's love interest, the fight is on! It's entertaining enough, but only in a "so bad that it's good" sort of way. The gorilla suit is horrible, and a flap on the back of the headpiece is clearly visible at all times. It actually looks to be a bear suit with a gorilla mask placed on it, considering it has claws and a slight tail. As for the mask, it is kept in a perpetual snarl, which of course, makes it much less realistic.

Two production stills from The Mighty Gorga *(1969).*

THE MIGHTY GORGA

The end of the 1960s saw two of the more shoddy gorilla suit movies. The first was the misleadingly titled *King of Kong Island* (1968), in which a mad scientist uses a mind control device to make gorillas do his bidding. In fact, in Italy, where the movie was produced, the story is set in Kenya, and the film is called *Eve, the Wild Woman*. As was common back then, a U.S. distributor took the movie, dubbed it into English, and gave it a new, more marketable title.

In 1969 came an independent film (that means a movie without a major studio behind it) called *The Mighty Gorga*. The movie is a loving tribute to *King Kong* which is held back by a truly terrible gorilla suit. This would be okay if the movie was a comedy, but it was shot as a serious film. The film focuses on explorer Mark Remington who decides to trek to Africa, where he has heard reports of a giant ape in the jungle that he hopes to capture. There he meets April Adams, daughter of the man who first reported the beast. Mark teams with April to find both her father and the gorilla, though on their trail is rival hunter Dan Morgan. While trekking through the jungle, the duo is attacked by a Tyrannosaurus Rex, which is fought away by the giant ape, Gorga. Mark shoots Gorga with a tranquilizer, but April feels sorry for the beast and removes a splinter from its hand. The duo is captured by natives who worship Gorga. In their village, they find Tonga Jack, April's father, and the trio escapes. Going through a cave system, they find the lost treasure of King Solomon but it is guarded by a dragon. A volcano erupts, killing the dragon and they escape back to the outside world where they are confronted by Morgan. At the last moment, they are saved from Morgan by Gorga and decide to let the giant ape go free.

SCHLOCK!

In 1973 came a movie that acknowledged how bad its ape suit actually was: *SCHLOCK!* Made in only 12 days for $60,000, this was the directorial debut of John Landis. Famous effects man Rick Baker made the molds for the suit in his mother's oven, and as stated earlier in the book, Landis actually played the ape!

SCHLOCK's tagline went, "A love stranger than King Kong! A monster more powerful than Godzilla!" And indeed, there are some *King Kong*-type elements in the film, such as the ape absconding with a girl to the top of a building where he is shot at by police. After the success of *Animal House*, Jack Harris re-released the film as *The Banana Monster* and made sure to create a new trailer based on John Landis's more recent success.

The film's best scene is easily the one where the monster ape walks into a movie theater. There patrons assume he's a man in a costume, when in fact he's a dangerous animal!

KING KONG RIP-OFFS

In 1975, Italian producer Dino De Laurentiis announced his intention to remake *King Kong*. This set off a bevy of imitators being announced, such as *Attack of the Giant Apes*, *Kongorilla*, and Roger Corman's *King Kong*. None of these ever got made, by the way, but quite a few others did. The first of these was a movie eventually released as *A*P*E*, but that wasn't the movie's original title. It was first announced as "The New King Kong" and later "Super Kong."

Ad for A*P*E *noting that it is not to be confused with* King Kong.

When threatened by a lawsuit by Dino De Laurentiis, the producers renamed the movie *A*P*E,* short for "**A**ttacking **P**rimate Monst**E**r." The movie was shot in 3-D over two weeks in South Korea on an effects budget of only $1,200.

The movie begins on a ship at sea, where a recently captured ape is being transported to Disneyland. The ape bursts free from the cargo ship and battles a giant great white shark in the water in a nod to the movie *Jaws* from 1975. The ape then swims to South Korea, where it tramples across the countryside. Marilyn Baker (Joanna Kerns of TV's *Growing Pains*), an actress making a film in South Korea, is eventually abducted by the huge ape during shooting. During a military strike, Marilyn is rescued by her beau, a reporter named Tom. Marilyn is taken to the home of a Korean general in Seoul for safe keeping. The huge ape tracks her down and captures her again. The military attacks the ape once again and it dies as Marilyn watches in tears.

Though *A*P*E* was shot as though it was a serious movie, other productions were smarter and decided to make their Kong rip-offs as spoofs. The best-known of these is easily *Queen Kong*, in which a female ape abducts a handsome actor!

In the story, an all-female film crew is making a jungle adventure when the male lead quits. The main producer, Luce Habit, roams the streets of London until she finds her ideal man: Ray Fay (get it, a reversal of the name Fay Wray?). Habit brings the dimwitted Ray to Africa to resume shooting and there they discover a mysterious tribe that worships a giant ape, whom Ray is given to as an offering. The ape, Queen Kong, becomes infatuated with Ray and defends him from several dinosaur attacks in the jungle. Eventually, Ray is rescued by Habit and her crew, who also knock out Queen Kong. Habit tows Queen Kong back to London, where she is put on display.

When the ape becomes angered at the treatment of Ray during a live show, she breaks free of her restraints and goes on the rampage. Climbing atop Big Ben with Ray, Queen Kong is besieged by helicopters and jets until Ray gives an impassioned speech on women's rights. The government calls off their attack and Queen Kong is allowed to return to Africa.

Another lesser-known spoof from the same time was *King Kung Fu*, about a karate-chopping gorilla! During the climax, the ape climbs the tallest building in town, the Holiday Inn, with a beautiful girl and fights a helicopter (in stop motion no less) which is fairly amusing. Just when we think it's going to end in tragedy and the ape falls, he lands on the helicopter (safely between the top and rear blades). And, in the very final scene, he commandeers and flies off in the same helicopter. Filmed entirely in Wichita, Kansas, the troubled production began in 1974, ran out of money, started up again, and finished principal photography by 1976.

Not all the Kong "rip-offs" were bad, though. Some were quite good and original in their own right. *Yeti: Giant of the 20th Century* tells the story of a brother and sister who discover a giant, frozen abominable snowman. However, the snowman isn't abominable at all and is quite friendly. Or friendly until he is put on display and becomes mistreated, that is. Then he becomes angry and trashes a major city. Happily though, unlike Kong, the Yeti is allowed to live at the film's end, and he returns to the icy glacier where he was found.

Even better was *Mighty Peking Man*, from the Shaw Brothers in Hong Kong. In the movie, a crew of Chinese anthropologists journeys into the Himalayan Mountains in hopes of finding a legendary giant known as the Mighty Peking Man. When the party of explorers abandons one of their own, Johnny Feng, the lone anthropologist ends up discovering the giant ape and also a jungle girl raised by the monster named Samantha. As Johnny and Samantha fall in love, Johnny convinces her and her giant pet to travel with him to civilization. Things take a turn for the worse when Johnny's partners begin exploiting Mighty Peking Man, who grows angry and escapes in Hong Kong. Samantha and Johnny do their best to save the giant ape, who has climbed atop a skyscraper, but it is to no avail and the beast is pummeled with bullets, some of which also hit Samantha. Mighty Peking Man falls to his death as Johnny scoops up an unconscious Samantha in his arms, her fate uncertain.

Despite the downbeat ending, *Mighty Peking Man* is a fun movie with colorful effects scenes. The miniatures were created by Sadamasa Arikawa, a former special effects director for the Japanese Godzilla movies. The film was released in the U.S. in 1980 under the new title *Goliathon*.

Still of the Hong Kong miniature set in **Mighty Peking Man** *(1977).*

Still from Bye, Bye Monkey *(1978).*

KONG CAMEOS

Even movies not centered around giant apes from the 1970s managed to squeeze in nods to King Kong. The strangest by far is the French art film *Bye, Bye Monkey* (1978). For that film, the leftover scale body prop from the 1976 *King Kong* was used to represent a giant dead ape found on a beach. A man named Lafayett finds a baby chimp hanging around the body and adopts it! But, the movie really isn't about King Kong or apes despite how it begins.

In Taiwan was produced a movie called *The Merciful Buddha* (1979), which has a scene of a giant ape. This fairy tale type story begins with just that, a fairy tale from the village elder explaining the complicated mythology of the monkey village. The man says that when the eye of the monkey on the mountain turns to gold, that means prosperity will befall the village. When the eye of the monkey turns red, that means disaster will befall the village.

One day it turns red and the mountain begins to move—and from it emerges a shoddy ape suit. Then, the ape suit doesn't even wreck the village! Instead, it quickly transforms into a baby chimp, and natural disasters proceed to destroy the village instead. In the film's last few moments, we do briefly see the chimp again, which grows gigantic and is reabsorbed into the mountain very quickly.

Much more fun was 1977's *Where Time Began*, a Spanish adaptation of Jules Verne's *Journey to the Center of the Earth*. In this iteration, one of the prehistoric creatures encountered at the earth's center is a giant ape. The giant ape figures into the climax where it chases the two romantic leads through a petrified forest. When they hide in the hollow of a tree, the giant ape uproots it. Overall, the suit for the ape is much better than the one used for *A*P*E* around the same time and is about on par with *Mighty Peking Man*.

One of the last movies produced to feature a traditional man in an ape suit came from Japan. The film is called *The Ivory Ape*. It was produced by Tsuburaya Productions, the creators of TV's popular *Ultraman* series. The co-producers on the film were Rankin/Bass, the company behind such classics as *Rudolph the Red Nosed Reindeer* (1964).

The story concerns a rare, albino gorilla that is captured by farmers in Africa. Aubrey Raines, an evil big game hunter, comes and takes it away by boat. On his trail is a primatologist, Lil, and her associate, Baxter, a special agent from the department of the interior that deals in animal trafficking. When the ivory ape kills a man and escapes the

ship, which has docked in Bermuda, Baxter calls in Mark Kazarian (Jack Palance), a retired big game hunter, to capture the beast. However, Kazarian is lead to believe they want the ape dead, while Baxter and Lil do their best to capture it alive. As the ape is hunted it kills three men including Raines. The ape is tracked to a church by a mob. At the last moment, Kazarian realizes that the ape has given birth and begs everyone not to shoot. It is too late—another hunter fires off a shot. The ape dies, and Baxter finds a baby ape in its arms—but not of the rare albino variety. The last white ape is dead.

THE FUTURE

As special effects continue to progress with animatronics and a strange new art called computer animation (as seen 1982's *Tron*), the future is uncertain whereas the use of ape suits in movies go— and giant apes in general. There have been rumblings of sequels to the 1976 *King Kong* movie for some time now. Ideas pitched so far have Kong revived by science and another even has him fighting the Killer Whale from *Orca* (1977)! Whatever the future holds for giant apes, audiences everywhere look forward to their return to the big screen.

THE BIG BOOK OF JAPANESE GIANT MONSTER MOVIES SERIES

VOLUME 1: 1954-1982

VOLUME 2: 1984-2017

THE LOST FILMS

TERROR OF THE LOST TOKUSATSU FILMS

WRITING JAPANESE MONSTERS

EDITING JAPANESE MONSTERS

KONG UNMADE: THE LOST FILMS OF SKULL ISLAND

Be sure to read these other great books!

www.ingramcontent.com/pod-product-compliance
Lightning Source LLC
Chambersburg PA
CBHW081237080526
44587CB00022B/3973